Sincerely,
  Katie & Liv

© 2017 Liv Fagerholm and Katie Burbank

Published by Sungold Editions
www.sungoldeditions.com

Cover image: Liv Fagerholm

ISBN-13: 978-0-9991678-0-9

Poems by

Liv Fagerholm & Katie Burbank

Photos by

Liv Fagerholm

Sungold Editions • Santa Barbara
2017

Contents

Half Wilding	8
My Goddess	9
The Pussycat	10
More	11
Hummingbird Sunrise	12
First World-White Girl	13
Thick	15
A Poem for Israel	16
Twenty Year Sleep	17
How Do I Raise My Son?	18
For Mom	19
Inside Out	20
Workhorses	21
You Lost	22
Love Hurts	23
Honest	24
In the Crosshairs	25
I Love You, Oops!	26
Early Bird	27
I Didn't Wear a Bra Today	28
Red Suburbans	29
Breakable Warrior	30
Ode to the Tomato	31
The Wind Whispered	32
My Mother is the Moon	33
I Don't Need No Stinking Day	34
My Father's Land	35
Mr. Brown and Son	36
Mean Old Men	37
Elucidate	38
Alegria Resureccion' "Joy Resurrected"	41
Depression	42

This poetry book is dedicated to Tom.
Father and brother, he saw this before we did:
thanks for your love and support.

And to our wonderfully diverse and creative family,
who support our art unequivocally, thank you.
We love you too.

Katie

Half Wilding

I feel the shift within:
tectonic, subterranean.
Blowing my coat,
sly and wary.
Shape changing,
half wilding am I.
Eye on your throat,
walking with the Windigo.
Only half wildings know
to build a fire is to survive:
to run with wolves is to be alive.

LIV

My Goddess

She shines like the full moon
on a clear night
bathing the earth with
her loving night light
like a lotus she rose
from the muddiest water
spinning into beauty
on the wheel of God's potter
a hard knock life
doesn't prevent her from perfuming
the world with her love
that is always blooming

KATIE

The Pussycat

Where is my owl
in a beautiful pea-green boat
to wrap me in honey,
and a five pound note

Sing to me with a small guitar
take me sailing to lands afar
tell me how my beauty shows
for a year and a day
where the bong-tree grows

And there in the wood
Owl and Pussycat stood
looking up to the stars above
oh Pussycat my love

Feed me quince from a runcible spoon
dance with me by the light of the moon, the moon
hand in hand, on the edge of the sand
the Owl and the Pussycat
did just that

LIV

More

In becoming night
the quiet turns still
and stillness into silence.
Darkness becomes black.
My breasts
flood with pain,
my arms ache
at the thought of putting you down
for the night.

My heart beats
because I love you
my pulse is loud.
I didn't hold
you enough,
read to you
enough,
love you
enough today.

My throat tightens
and my eyes sting
at the remembered sound
of your giggle;
the brilliance of your smile.

My son, my beautiful baby boy.
tomorrow, I will hold you more,
love you more, read more, sing more, more, just more.

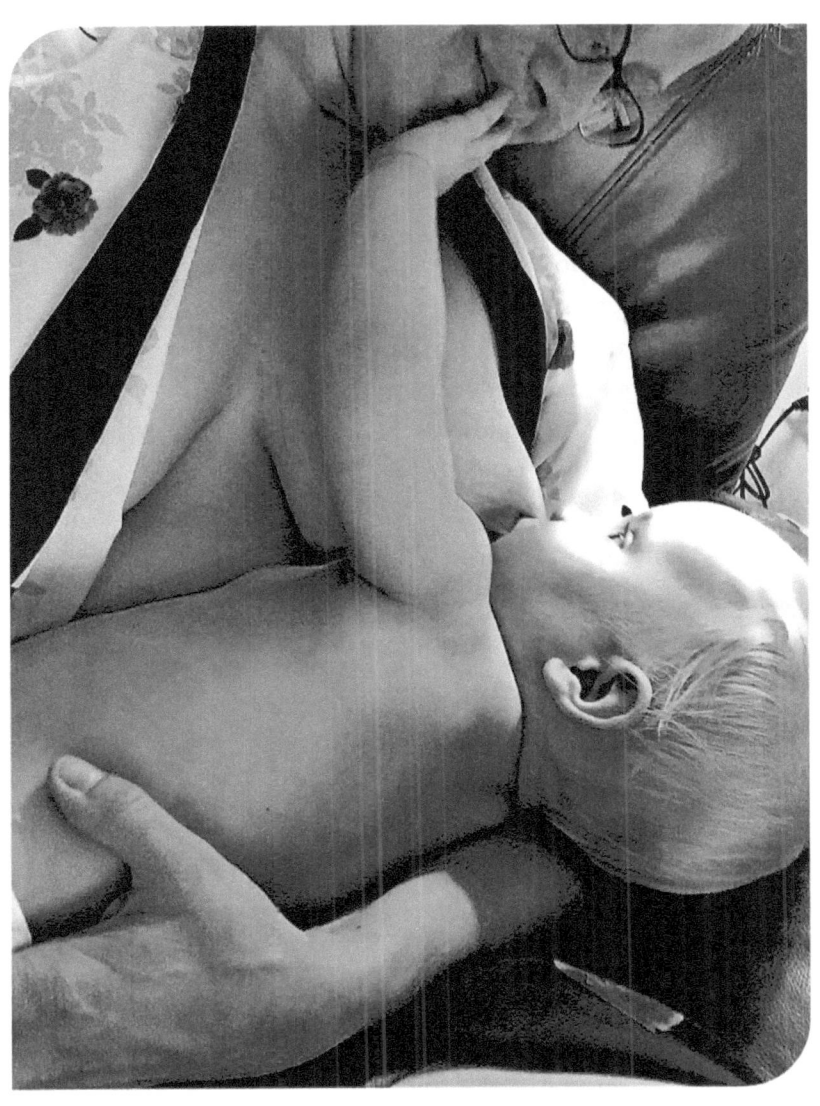

Katie

Hummingbird Sunrise

A hummingbird sunrise
ruby throated sun kissing
the dark breast of Earth
ruffled clouds above
moving so fast, as to be still
my beating heart,
will not forget to remember.
The beauty and surrender
of all ties.
Tender to my soul
is the hummingbird sunrise.

LIV

FIRST WORLD-WHITE GIRL

Sitting in the bathtub
soaking
in my son's Johnson's nighttime
bubble bath
reading Maya Angelou and her
phenomenal black girl problems.
I think about my white girl problems

Men have cheated on me
men have taken my money
told me I'm fat and they
didn't like my honey.

I was never a slave,
never called girl by a girl
younger than me.

I wish I was
a phenomenal woman
but, phenomenally, I don't believe myself
to be

sure, when I was a baby
someone misappropriated me.
But I'm a white girl;
strictly middle class.
The prejudices I feel are
mainly in my fat ass.
I'm a woman in a man's world
of course.

I may be obsessed
with my size—I can't lie
when I look in the mirror and see with my eyes
the Body before me
I'm overcome
it's phenomenal, the self-loathing.

I wish I was
a phenomenal woman.
But, phenomenally, I don't believe myself
to be.

Mostly I worry about my son
finding me dead on the bathroom
floor.
"She puked herself to death"
they'd say. "Bulimia
it's called" says another.
That's my white girl
problem.
Brought on by my first world
insecurities.

I wish I was
a phenomenal woman.
But, phenomenally, I don't believe myself
to be.

They'll give me a glass of water before I die
but I won't drink it before
stepping on
a man-made scale.
It's phenomenal.

Katie

Thick

Like a tree that grows, so does my torso.
Thick and solid, a testament to my knowledge
of culinary pleasure,
tendency towards leisure.
A rebel I am, I can't be happy thin.
I use my weight to tip the scales.
Disarm the adversaries, and throw the bales.
Scandinavian peasant by day, Venus by night.
I use my weight to push for right,
and everything else I believe in life.
Someday I'll be dead, but until then I can sit on your head.

LIV

A Poem for Israel

A country, where hope and desperation
live side by side.
Joy and hate dance entwined,
round the stone walls of Jerusalem.
Lines are fiercely drawn
in the dirt, air, consciousness
of the city, the country, the babies, the dead.

Israel, my beautiful country:
surpassing religion, surpassing belief.
I, a human, and you:
birthplace of mortal souls;
graveyard of human mercy.

Everywhere I step, breathe, and exist;
whispers mystic truths
that people travel from thousands of miles to hear.
Try to hear;
and evolution has made us deaf.

Oh, sweet Israel,
just a baby being quartered
between many mothers.
Where is King Solomon?
Where is the wise judge?

Alas, where there is human will
there is seldom any God.

Katie

Twenty Year Sleep

I fell asleep with the sun on my face,
children at my breast.
Strong and tall, my mind quick,
body full of strength, at its best.
Trouble came in dreams of loss,
loved ones hurt,
my boat by waves tossed.
Dark, huge bodies below me lurked.
One by one, took those I loved
alone in the murk,
torrents of rain from above.
Screaming, crying I held to the rope,
till beaten, head down,
without hope,
I heard the grate of hull on sand,
opened blue eyes to a foreign land.
The people were kind and gave me respite.
But, Oh! My heart would not let me forget
those I lost and gave up for dead.
At last I woke, twenty years gone by.
No longer young, no longer spry.
The children at my breast now have their own,
and don't remember the ones I have known.
How can it be, where did I go?
Into the deep, during my twenty year sleep.

LIV

How Do I Raise My Son?

How do I raise my son
to be an honorable man?
It's easy to say, don't cheat,
don't lie, don't hit, don't rape,
don't disrespect.

But many men have been told those don'ts
and did them anyways.

How do I raise my son
to be an honorable man?
It's easy to say, I didn't marry
your daddy cuz he did this and this and this.

But many men have been told what daddy did
and did them anyways:

How do I raise my son?
With kindness, with compassion,
with mutual respect. With
laughter and silliness; a love of animals and the moon.

The men who did them anyways
were not told that their feelings were ok.

Katie

For Mom

Still.
The day was sunny, felt chilled.
Thought I was strong, but wasn't.
Thought I knew, but didn't.
A week to try, a week to die.
Couldn't leave, wouldn't stay.
Cracked open, yet sealed.
Comforted, like torture
tried forgetting, afraid I won't remember.
Long time past, like yesterday.
I let go, but hold on... still.

LIV

Inside Out

The clouds are low on the mountaintop white
the aspens still shine sunny, yellow, and bright
the seasons converge:
fall is still hanging on.
Snowflakes will dance before the next dawn.
The cold is moving in with temperatures dropping
I've got my own in utero furnace and the flames will be popping.
My baby will be born when the spring shoots sprout.
Then my heart will be
on the inside out.

KATIE

WORKHORSES

We stamp our feet and shake our manes, like workhorses of old.
Brace our shoulders, settle into the load.
Strained harness creaking, titan hooves grind.
Muscles overcome inertia, but not time.
Momentum, scrambling legs in the moss, yanking roots, rubbing stumps, peeling bark off.
The load hangs on, at last to join the rest.
With a sure and smooth step, we turn and plod,
back into the forest.

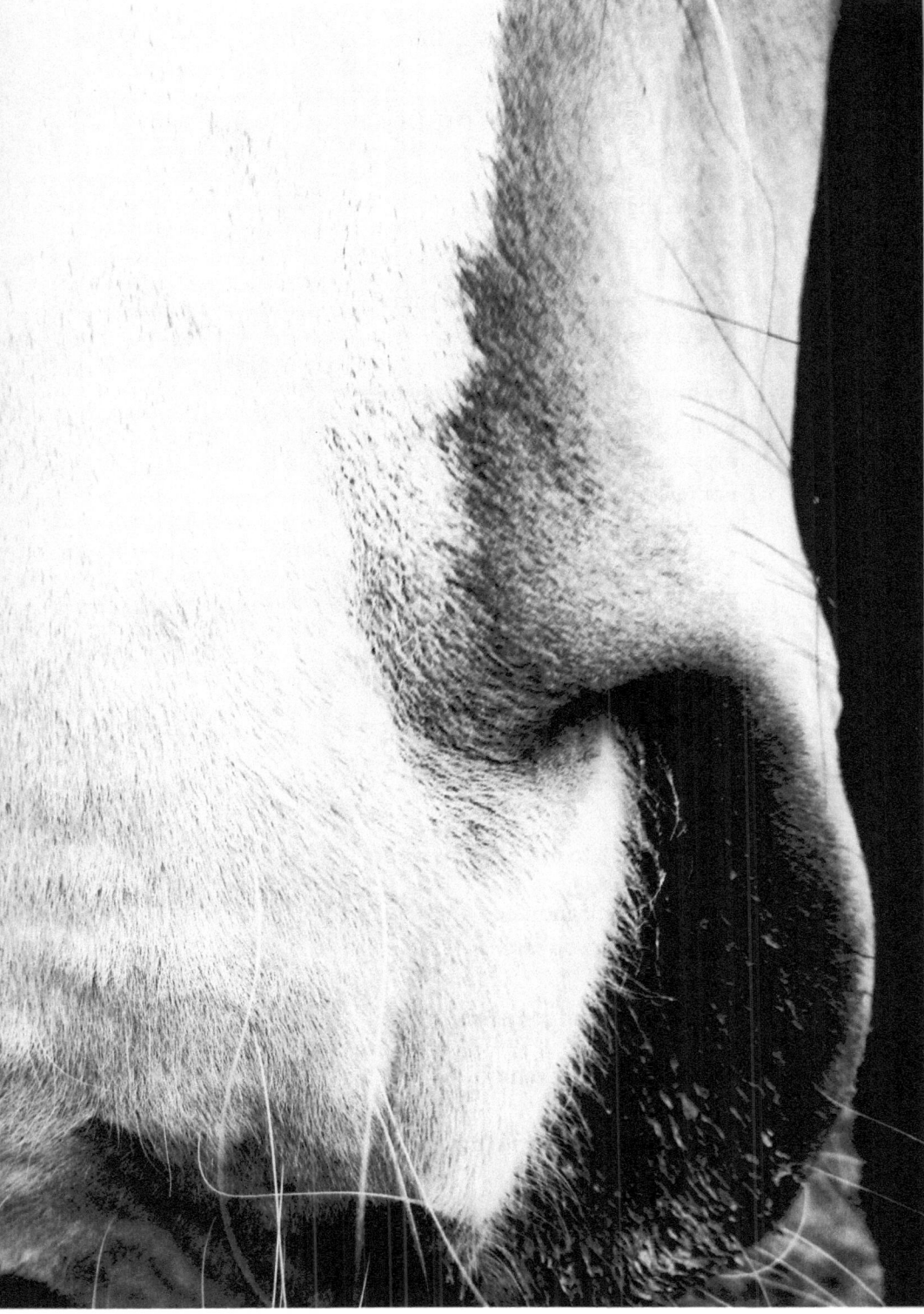

L iv

You Lost

blinded by your ignorance
and vanity
*
you'll never know how good I am
and was for you.
*
my brain is bigger than both my breasts
lumped together.
my pretty face was painted by god
not revlon or l'oreal.
my vagina is covered
by a natural mound of hair.
instead of clean shaven lips
like a 4yr old.
*
educated and smart
enough to know:
*
I deserve the love of one man.
a man
smart enough to make me his world.
*
unseeing from ignorance
you lost when you said,
"I guess
I'll see you round sometime."
*
distracted by your vanity
you don't know
I am the most beautiful thing
you've let go.

Katie

Love Hurts

It hurts to see you slow,
gaunt of flank, chin of snow.
Don't leave me like the others before,
always alone.
It hurts to touch you, feel the bones beneath, warmed yet by the heart below.
How can I let you go?
All the times, all the memories?
You come to me for a palliative caress, trying to ignore the duress of living, of breathing, of being alive.
How sweet to rest.
Love hurts, love bleeds…
Love hurts.

LIV

Honest

You were honest.
I didn't want to hear
and I offered
my heart up to you
like a sacrificial lamb
even as I said,
"no problem,
let's just hang out,
no strings attached."
"I'm a commitment-phobe."
you said
as I kissed you.
"I don't want to date."
you said
as I told you how much I cared for you.
"I don't want a girlfriend."
you said
as I put your hand to my breast.
"I have a friend in MO I sleep with."
you said.
as I fed you pieces of my heart.
"Chew" I said.

Katie

In the Crosshairs

Something snapped inside me today.
Whether it was the guns or women in the crosshairs, I cannot say.
But I vow right now my granddaughters will never face that hate…
    somehow—someway.
I get it, I really do. I've tried understanding, loving, listened to
    their point of view.
There is a knowing that comes from within and provides a
compass—the true north… that sureness of justice and right.
This isn't it, not even close.
It's scary to know some people will kill, exercising their second
    amendment right.
But, I refuse to be silent and be a good girl, this unarmed warrior
    is prepared to fight.

LIV

I Love You, Oops!

I'm afraid I'll blurt out
I love you
I don't think
I love you
I think
I love
The you I want
You to be:
The one I love.

Katie

Early Bird

I miss him most on Sunday morning,
when all is quiet.
A smirk, a smile, a brisk shave in the sink.
I never saw a bird take a better bath, I think.

White boxers sagging over a flat ass.
a creak of the floor, squeak of the chair.
Diesel engine starting in cold air.

Pickup campers and old friends,
tagging along with sandy feet.
Down to George's for a beer,
orange crush for me.

I think of him when I rub my feet…just like he.
Or, smirk and smile and think of something funny,
only to me.

Sometimes I forget…think I have to rush.
But, then I remember and
my voice sinks to a hush.

I miss him most on Sunday morning when all is quiet.

LIV

I Didn't Wear a Bra Today

I let it all hang loose.
I undid the hooks and let it fall,
then kicked it with my boots.
I'm going to let them hang—
enjoy them jiggle when I'm walking.
Ask me how the weather is,
I'll let my nipples do the talking.
Bing Crosby sings, "Don't fence me in"
my breasts have sung likewise.
So now they view the jaded grass
instead of the monotonous skies.

Katie

Red Suburbans

Red Suburbans and white vans,
from the corner of my eye.
Creaky leaf springs, diesel exhaust, Mopar engine… gone and lost.
No more afternoon rides,
sunshine and ice cream running down the sides.
Life was free, and so were we.
Hard to believe it was really me,
and you…you make three.

Red Suburbans and white vans from the corner of my eye,
Haunting my memories and making me cry.
Follow the finger like a divining rod,
to apple blossoms and misty ponds.
Endless farm fields strain the eye…
as red Suburbans and white vans drive by.

LIV

Breakable Warrior

I am a warrior who isn't unbreakable;
I am a goddess with body image issues;
and a really good mother who uses a lot of tissues.

I am woman who roars but isn't sure what bra size I wear.

I am a writer who doesn't always know how to write;
I am an artist who can't get the pictures out of my head;
a retired dancer whose body has already been bled.

I am a woman who roars but isn't sure what bra size I wear.

I am a daughter that doesn't do anything you say;
I am a rebel spirit that doesn't stay up too late;
a fighter who doesn't always win the fight.

I am a woman who roars but isn't sure what bra size I wear.

KATIE

ODE TO THE TOMATO

Oh tomato how I love you so!

I wait and wait until you're ripe,
then eat till my underwear has a stripe.
Tomatoes here, tomatoes there,
I can't afford more underwear.
I dry, purée, and I chop…
still you grow and won't stop.

Tomato of mine I can't keep up,
(a few have sailed over the roof top!)
some hid in the peppers,
and some died on the spot.
Till next year, my love,
I will give you a shove…

Corn, corn how I love you so…
Wait, I didn't have corn!

LIV

THE WIND WHISPERED

Yesterday at the beach the
wind whispered the poetry of the
ocean in my ear, the
ocean said 'move to my sandy shores and
raise your son on my waves.
We will teach him of light and love,
of darkness and danger,
of safety and serenity.'

'Trust my waters to
lap up your tears,
wave at your joys,
and carry you on my surf.'

Yesterday at the beach the
wind whispered the poetry of the
ocean in my ear, the
ocean said 'move to my sandy shores and
raise your son on my waves.

Katie

My Mother is the Moon

My mother is the moon, she watches over me.
Sometimes a crescent moon over the silo at night so I can see.
My mother is a wildflower that grows in the cool, green woods
with very little show.
My mother is a soft, warm quilt,
with all the colors of my life in it.
My mother is the moon, she watches over me.

LIV

I Don't Need No Stinking Day

I don't need no stinking day
I know what I am worth
I grew you in my body, boy,
Mother Nature birthed this earth

Without women your ego
would have no one to dominate
our legs give you wet dreams
and don't tell me to lose weight.

Without women you'd have
no one to fertilize
no one to kiss your boo boos
no one to sympathize.

Don't placate me with
a special woman's day
change your words, your voice
change what you think and say.

I will roar & roar & roar
until my words are respected
don't give me a fucking day
and then support the current elected.

Katie

My Father's Land

I had to leave
my father's land
I had to learn to grow like
my father's land
I had to make my fortune far from
my father's land

I learned my heart is in
my father's land
to nurture and watch over
my father's land
so my children and their children will know
my father's land

LIV

Mr. Brown and Son

One I never knew
he speaks to me through you
his son, I did know
and of him there are too few.

Both of them were kind
each had a brilliant mind
gentle giants
their two spirits now reassigned

God, grant us the grace
to know their spiritual face
let them guide us
to your ultimate embrace.

Katie

Mean Old Men

Mean old men think they know
what is best for me.
What I should keep—
what I should grow.
Fingering me as a culprit—
accosting me in private.
Insulting me with patronizing tones.
I decide what I can stand—
I decide what's best for me,
and their poison will not come to be.

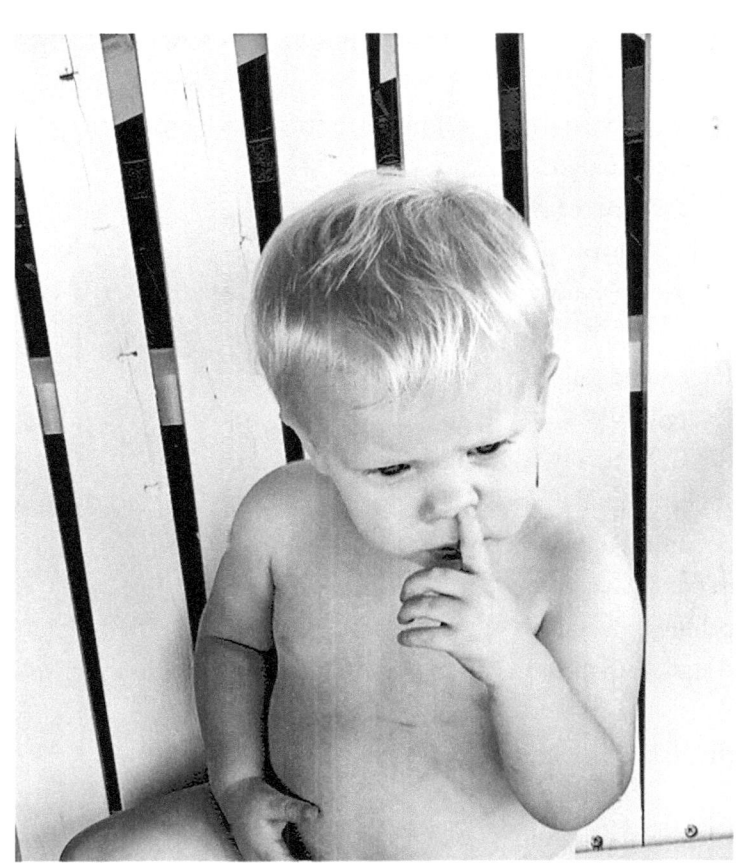

Liv

Elucidate

Let me elucidate: This isn't the world
I planned on raising my son in. The world where I excitedly tell him
you were born during a time of our first black president, which heralded
a movement of peace and acceptance,
and when you were
almost 2 we elected our first female president.

I imagined telling my son,
excitedly:
the US is finally realizing its true self.
we have finally
become a nation
of equality, a nation of acceptance, a nation of
pride in diversity.
A nation that stands up to bullies; helps the poor as much as it does
the rich.

Let me elucidate:
that isn't the world we live in.

On the day my son turned 2,
I cried in joy at his beautifulness, I cried in heartbreak at the world he is growing up in.

In less time
than it takes to shave my legs, the world was taken over
by an orange swine
preaching hate, screaming pussy, and inspiring acts
of racism and violence.

His brash and brazen
carelessness has given permission to those
whose insecurities
breed evil, fear, and unfounded loathing.

Let me elucidate:
this is not the world I planned on
raising my son in.

We live in a world
where Maya Angelou, Alice Walker, and Langston Hughes
are still relevant
today…
Their works and words should be testament to the history of our
country
not the current atmosphere.
But here we are,
reading
the same words from the 20's, 30's, 40's, 50's and 60's
and they still read
true and truer. It might as well have been
penned today.

Let me elucidate:
we are back to the beginning.

I am afraid for my child.
because he is white, because he is privileged and
because his current
political male examples are everything I stand against.
God forbid
he thinks it's ok to treat any one as less than.
God forbid he
believes a word of the 45th, whose name burns my tongue.

God give me the grace
to teach him the kind of kindness
that withstands
the constant battle of fear, won't be worn down by
bitterness and panic.
Like a river rock refusing to be worn down by the unrelenting
river.

Katie

Alegria Resureccion' "Joy Resurrected"

Pirate eyes gleam with turquoise dreams.
Trapped below or tied to the mast,
struggling against bonds yet unseen.
Atop the swell, a glimpse of life,
with joy resurrected, no strife in sight.
Ebbing, flowing, massaging, rolling,
debriding crustaceans from a past life.
Barnacles of the soul fall below to
Poseidon's embrace.
The moon draws the tide, and sets the pace.
Disintegration, reformation, resurrection for thee.
Roaring on the surface, but quiet underneath.
Like a pirate, plundering what thee needs,
with joy resurrected by the sea.

LIV

Depression

When the mountains can't solace my riven heart
when my son's smile can't formidably tear us apart.

I know I have fallen
into despondence

the hole of melancholia is so incredibly deep
deeper than the length of my veins through which my blood seeps

please let my baby's blue eyes
reflect love in me

the den of self-loathing is a welcome reprieve
to the effort it takes to love someone like me

I beg you to undo this pain

the light of the greatest thing I've ever birthed in my life
inspires me to get up every morning like a 1950's dutiful wife

I beg: may I be happy, please may I know peace.

I'm desperate to know self love and live inspired
for myself and my son: please god reignite my inner fire.

I plead: may I be free from suffering.

About the Authors

Liv M. Fagerholm

Raised just north of Seattle, Liv spent her 20's terrorizing downtown Seattle with friends having Disco dress up parties and body painting to Michael Jackson's Thriller, until she moved to beautiful Colorado where she finally found her adult home nestled in the Rocky Mountains. Liv loves her son, her boxer dog, yoga, mountains, mermaids, Harry Potter, and the Oxford comma. An English Major from the University of Washington, she still doesn't know what she wants to be when she grows up and finds solace in NPR's Wait, Wait, Don't Tell Me and Garrison Keillor's A prairie Home Companion. She writes poetry to find direction and purpose but also to be able to say F&^* in a pretty way.

Katie Burbank

The youngest of six kids, Katie was born and raised a farm girl who thought she was a Native American in Rochester, Minnesota. She is the mother of 3 grown kids, has a giant hunk of burning love for a husband, and often feels like a fat white woman trapped in the body of a fat white woman. Katie dreams of being Pocahontas and a poet laureate. Until then, she's a lusty reader of the Outlander series, and was a fan before it became a TV show, works as a genetics nurse, and maintains her own farm filled with chickens, horses, cats, dogs, kids, and grandkids.

www.ingramcontent.com/pod-product-compliance
Lightning Source LLC
Chambersburg PA
CBHW020625300426
44113CB00007B/787